Rent to Own
Solution

—————— TO ——————

Home
Ownership

For good people who have been turned down for a
mortgage by the big banks and mortgage companies

By JON SIMCOE
and DAVE DUBEAU

The Rent to Own Solution to Home Ownership

ISBN-13: 978-0-9964460-2-0
ISBN-10: 0-9964460-2-8

Published by: Expert Author Publishing
http://expertauthorpublishing.com

Canadian Address:
501- 1155 The High Street,
Coquitlam, BC, Canada
V3B.7W4
Phone: (604) 941-3041
Fax: (604) 944-7993

US Address:
1300 Boblett Street
Unit A-218
Blaine, WA 98230
Phone: (866) 492-6623
Fax: (250) 493-6603

Contents

Common Rent to Own Mistakes, Challenges, and Traps(And How to Avoid Them)

Introduction

A good life is measured in many ways. It's measured in love, family and friends. It's measured in memories, laughter, and joy. It's also measured in terms of success, happiness, financial security and stability.

There's one thing that connects all of these things...

A home.

A home is the symbol of a good life.

Your home is a place where you can be surrounded by love, family, and friends.

It's a place where you're able to create lasting memories. These memories aren't just yours. They belong to your family and children, too.

A home keeps you safe and provides your family with a sense of security that cannot be obtained by any other means. It's your haven.

A home represents stability, success, and financial security.

For many good, hard-working and deserving Canadians the dream of owning a home feels out of reach.

Why Good People Don't Qualify For Mortgages:

There are many reasons why good, deserving families don't qualify for mortgages to buy their own homes.

In today's financial environment, the big banks and finance companies are very picky about whom they will lend money to in order to buy a home.

Here are some of the reasons you might not qualify for a mortgage...

You may have credit 'glitches' from past mistakes.

Sometimes the mistakes of our youth (or any stage of our lives) follow us for a long time. If you have been irresponsible with your credit in the past, then unless you actively work to clean it up, the record of that can stick with you for a long time into the future. That cell phone bill you forgot to pay, the credit cards you paid late, the little electricity bill that went into collections... those all add up and can KILL your credit score very quickly.

You have gone through bankruptcy.

Hey, life happens. Sometime the debt gets too big to be able to handle, and good people are forced into bankruptcy. It could be for any number of reasons... losing a job, getting sick (or a loved one getting sick), an unsuccessful business venture, etc.

Whatever the reason, going bankrupt is a huge red flag for banks and lenders, and they won't touch you for several years after you've been cleared (discharged), and then ONLY if you are 'squeaky clean' with your credit and payment history.

You are self-employed.

So you've decided to take control of your financial future and go into business for yourself! Congratulations! However, the banks don't look very favorably upon the self-employed... at least not for the first few years that you are in business. Banks want to see at least 2 years of SOLID (i.e. profitable) business growth before they will give you a loan or credit.

(It always strikes me as funny that they look so favorably upon people who are employees and can be fired/laid off at any moment... but look down their noses at self-employed people).

Plus... one of the 'benefits' of being self employed is that you can legitimately minimize your income by claiming a lot of expenses as business expenses. That's great for lowering your tax bill, but not so great for getting a mortgage from the banks.

Nowadays the banks look at your income you claim for taxes to determine how much (if any) money they will lend you.

You are a recent immigrant to the country.

Welcome to Canada! Good luck getting a mortgage unless you have a LOT of cash in your pockets. New immigrants start afresh in Canada, and that means that the banks want to see them establish some credit history before they will loan them any money to buy a home. This usually means that you will have to work at it for 1-2 years in order to build up enough credit to qualify for a mortgage.

You don't have enough credit history.

Perhaps you grew up in a household that believes "only buy something when you have the cash to buy it" and you have avoided credit at all costs.

That is a very admirable quality, and it has probably done you a great service as far as keeping you out of debt and NOT having to pay ridiculous amounts of interest to credit card companies and other lenders.

However, it is very hard to save up all the cash you need to buy a home for $300,000 to $700,000 (depending on where you live)!

And by not having ever borrowed any money, gotten a loan, or used a credit card in the past, the banks and lenders cannot see what kind of a 'borrower' you are. Even though you have zero debt and have been super-responsible with your money... they don't care!

To them, you are a big risk... because you are an 'unknown.'

So before you can qualify to get a mortgage, they want to see how you behave with other, smaller loans and credit. They want to know for certain that you are going to pay your bills, and pay them in a timely fashion.

So those are some of the most common reasons that good people, just like you and your family, may not qualify for a mortgage right now with the big banks and their super-tight lending criteria.

But don't lose heart! There is a solution. And that's what this short book is all about.

Have you heard the saying, "Where there is a will, there is a way?"

It's true. If you have the will to own a home, there really is a way. Over the next XX pages you'll discover the many benefits of owning your own home. We'll talk about the options and paths available to you as well as the steps you can begin taking right away to realize your dream of home ownership.

We'll show you how to protect yourself from bad deals and we'll also talk about how the steps you take today can help secure a strong financial future for you and your loved ones.

Owning a home opens up a world of opportunities to you. So let's get started!

*There is something permanent,
and something extremely profound,
in owning a home.*

Kenny Guinn

The 9 BIGGEST Reasons to Own Your Home Instead of Renting

Let's take a look at what the BIGGEST Benefits of owning your own home are, and we'll start with something I think you will really 'appreciate.'

Reason #1
Real Estate Appreciates in Value Over the Long Term

D o you like to make money? How about making money for just living in your own house? Nice!

Most people enjoy making money, especially when they're able to use leverage and earn money on their investments. Let's say you invest one hundred dollars today and ten years from now that small investment is worth $1,000.

Not bad, right?

It's enough to motivate anyone to start saving and investing.

Owning a home is a unique opportunity to earn money on an investment – an investment that you actually live in and use every day!

Why?

Because Real Estate (your home) Appreciates in Value Over Time

Historically in Canada, real estate always increases in value over time. The $300,000 home you buy today may very well be worth more than $400,000 in five to ten years.

Yes, that's a $100,000 increase in the value of your property.

That's not a made up number; that's the reality.

According to the Canadian Real Estate Association, on average, homes appreciate 3 percent a year in most cities across the country.

This is unique to real estate. Most things you purchase depreciate in value after you buy them. The moment you take possession, they begin losing value. For example, when you buy a new car and drive it off the lot, it can immediately lose one third of its value.

That $20,000 car is now worth $15,000 or less. OUCH! And that's the reality for most purchases.

Unlike Most Things You Buy, Real Estate Increases in Value

When you rent, your money is going into your landlord's pocket. You're not making one red cent. When you buy a home, not only are you getting many other amazing benefits, you're growing your money and enjoying the ability to enjoy the profits of your appreciating property.

At a Glance

- When you buy a home, the home increases in value over time – it appreciates.

- Your investment multiplies and grows.

- You can make money while making memories in your home.

- When you rent, you're giving your hard-earned cash to your landlord. When you buy, you're making an investment and making more money over the long run.

OK, now that we know we can make money from just living in our own home, let's look at one of the 'emotional' benefits of owning your own home.

Reason #2
The Pride and Satisfaction of Home Ownership

There's nothing like owning your own home. Not only are you able to find the peace and comfort that's not always available in a rental (you can't control who the new tenants are who move in near you)) you're able to enjoy the freedom and control of being a home owner.

Ownership gives you more freedom and control over your life. You are the person who makes the decisions and the rules.

- When you own your home, you are able to paint the walls the colors you want.

- You can plant the kind of garden you want.

- You are free to turn up the stereo or TV as loud as you want (within reason of course!)

- If you have children, they can decorate their rooms however they want. You may end up with purple walls and a yellow ceiling, but the choice is yours – or theirs in this case :-).

- You can take down walls, add windows and doors and make your home the place you've always wanted to live.

- You can do whatever you want to do with your home.

You can landscape and remodel however you like. You don't have to wait for permission.

You also don't have to wait for a landlord to fix something. If your dishwasher is broken, you can fix it yourself or call a repairperson who can fix it immediately. In rentals, it's not uncommon to have to wait days, if not weeks, for minor repairs.

You Take Pride in Your Home and Your Accomplishment

Freedom to make your home your castle is only the beginning. When you own your home, you take better care of it then when you rent it. Owning a home is an accomplishment and it's something to be proud of. This is especially true if you've struggled financially. Being able to recover from financial struggle and own a home is significant.

In fact, for many people it's the first sign of a successful life.

Even if you take great care of the place you rent, when you care for your own home there's an extra amount of pride and satisfaction that comes from it. (And it can pay off down the road too, but we'll talk about that in a bit.)

You'll invite people over more often. Your friends and family can come in from out of town and you'll want them to stay with you – well, it depends on your friends and family, but you get the point.

When you rent, the landlord owns the home and you have to follow their rules. It's their property and they're the ones who are benefitting from renting it to you. That's fine for them, but it's not very good for you.

So owning your own home means you will enjoy the pride of ownership. You can personalize it and make your house the home you've always wanted.

And perhaps as a side note, you never have to worry about the landlord selling your home out from under you after you've spent all that time and energy creating a home. (It does happen quite often to renters and it's heartbreaking.)

At a Glance

- Home ownership gives you control over the interior and exterior of your home.

- You can landscape as you'd like.

- You can own pets.

- You'll feel a sense of pride and accomplishment.

- You may take better care of it; it's an investment after all.

- No one can sell the home out from under you after you've made it yours.

Let's face it...most of us don't 'like' to save. We'd rather have fun and spend our money instead. When you are a home owner, your house is kind of like a piggy bank for your future.

Reason #3
Increasing Equity
Is Like a 'Forced' Savings Plan

Owning a home is a unique investment opportunity that renters simply do not have.

When you pay rent, the money you pay goes to the landlord. You never see a penny of your rent money again.

However, when you buy a home you are able to enjoy the benefits of having equity in your home. This equity can be leveraged in a number of different ways. We'll talk about those in a bit.

First, let's talk about how much money you will be building up as you enjoy the increasing equity in your home.

A Quick Look at the Concept of Home Equity

Home equity is the portion of your home that you actually own.

As you pay off the home and make mortgage payments to the bank, you'll earn what's referred to as equity.

When you buy a home, you make payments to the bank every month. Those payments are to pay the bank back for their loan to you to buy the home, aka your mortgage.

There are two parts to your monthly payment. One part of the payment is interest. It's the cost of the loan. It's what the bank charges you for using their money.

The other part of the payment is principal. It's the part of the payment that actually goes toward paying off the underlying loan amount on your home.

So each month you will make payments to both the interest portion of the loan as well as the principal portion.

Generally speaking, you'll pay more in interest in the beginning of your loan and you'll pay more principal later as the interest is paid off.

A Unique Opportunity

As we've discussed, your home will likely increase in value over time (appreciation). That means that your $350,000 home will most likely be worth $10,000, $20,000, or even $100,000 **more** than what you paid for it, at some point in the future.

The value of your property increases, which puts more money into your pocket. The value of your home is appreciating and your loan amount is declining.

Your equity is that difference between the property value and your outstanding loan amount. Therefore, you actually make money as you continue to pay off your mortgage!

Your Equity Continues to Increase – and that is like an Instant Savings Account

As you make payments AND as the property increases in value, your equity continues to rise. You can consider it as a type of savings account, where your house continues to appreciate, and your loan amount continues to decline.

You certainly can't say that about paying rent!

Ah, the different options you will have!

There are many different ways to make good use of your home equity. You can leverage it to make improvements on your home with a home equity loan. This means you're borrowing a portion of your home's equity. If you use the money to increase the value of your home, you are then actually making even more money.

For example, if you borrow $30,000 in a home equity loan and you remodel the kitchen, or put in a rental suite in the basement, that can increase the value of your home by $50,000.

You've made $20,000 by borrowing from your equity.

Invest in Other Opportunities

You can also use a portion of your equity to invest in something else. You can borrow against this equity in your home at a very low interest rate, and then you turn around and invest it in something that pays a higher rate. This way you actually make money on the bank's money. Wouldn't that be nice for a change?

Memories of a Lifetime

Some people have been known to use their home equity to pay for vacations, college tuition for their children, and for "stuff" like cars and material belongings. That's not always the best way to use the savings.

However, at the end of the day, it's your decision and your money. You get to decide what to do with the investment in your home. That's definitely not something that you can say when you rent.

At a Glance

- Owning a home is a unique investment opportunity.

- As you make payments on your mortgage, you pay off interest and the principal on the loan.

- As you pay off the loan, you earn equity.

- Appreciation also increases the equity.

- Equity is an instant savings account. It's money that you can use, invest, and capitalize on.

- You don't earn equity when you rent. It's strictly a benefit of home ownership.

The ache for home lives in all of us, the safe place where we can go as we are and not be questioned.

Maya Angelou

Have you ever found yourself in a financial 'jam' and with nowhere to turn for the money you needed? When you are a home owner, you can get access to cash FAST.

Reason #4
You Can Borrow Against Your Home Equity in an Emergency

We just talked about how you can borrow against your equity for home improvements. This is a nice way to make more money on your home.

Sometimes, though, it's not about making more money and building for your future.

Sometimes you need a little extra help dealing with what's happening right now.

Let's face it. Sh...tuff happens.

Most people don't have a sizable emergency savings account. Between paying bills, paying down debt, and saving for the things you need, building an emergency savings fund is at the bottom of the priority list.

When you own your own home, you have a *built-in emergency savings fund*.

Emergencies are Never Really Expected

They call them emergencies for a reason. You get into an accident. A tree falls on your house. You get sick. You lose a job or you have to travel to care for a loved one.

Life is full of little (or big) surprises, and when you're not financially prepared for them, they can wipe you out!

A little story....

Julie and her husband Frank didn't have a savings plan. They didn't own a house. Every penny they earned went toward their rent, bills, and paying down their debt.

Every little unexpected expense felt like an emergency. When the car needed a new clutch, they had to pay for it with credit or borrow money from family and friends. They didn't have the $1,000 necessary to pay for it.

These little emergencies added up and before long, Julie and Frank were deeper in debt and they felt completely unable to pull themselves out of the hole. They felt beaten down – like they'd never be able to save enough for a down payment on a house when they couldn't even get out of their debt situation.

Their story ends on a positive note. It took some diligence and a willingness to listen to an expert credit counselor, but today Frank and Julie do own their own home. Even better, they know that if life should surprise them with an emergency, they have their home equity to lean on.

Just that simple fact makes life much less stressful. When those emergencies pop up, and they do still happen, Julie and Frank don't feel stressed about them.

Timely Help in a Financial Bind

Your home equity gives you peace of mind. You can use it to manage financial emergencies. You'll find that when you know you have backup, you'll feel less stressed and better able to manage financial challenges.

And if you truly are in a tremendous financial bind and you need to borrow from your home equity, you can.

It's generally an easy, fast, and inexpensive process. You can use your home equity line of credit or a home equity loan to deal with your emergency and help get you out of your financial bind.

It keeps you out of credit card debt, your friends and family won't avoid your calls, and it gives you the peace of mind you need to keep moving forward and achieving your financial goals.

A Word of Caution...

Don't make the mistake that some people have made. Your home equity line of credit is NOT a personal ATM.

It's your emergency savings plan and backup just in case you need it. It should only be used when there's no other option. Constantly borrowing from your home's equity will bite you in the rear down the line.

It's still money that you'll need to pay back. Use it wisely and remember that if you are able to leave your equity untouched, or leverage it to make money, you're building wealth.

At a Glance

- Emergencies are a part of life.

- Emergencies can destroy your financial security.

- Home equity is an emergency back-up plan. You can borrow from your home equity when you really need to.

- It's not an ATM, but your home equity can be the comfort you need to alleviate financial stress.

*Real estate is truly an amazing investment.
Just think about it... if someone came to you and said
"Hey friend, I've got $30,000... will you please lend me
$300,000 to buy a house and I'll pay you back over the
next 30 years." What would you tell them? Probably a
big fat "No Way!" Thankfully the banks LOVE lending on
real estate, and that's why...*

Reason #5
A Home Is a Leveraged Investment Using Other People's Money

R eal estate provides an opportunity that you just can't really find anywhere else.

There's just no other investment where you can leverage so much of the bank's money for your own benefit.

Why do banks loan you money? What's in it for them?

Banks lend out money on mortgages because they earn interest. It's that simple.

Let's say you want to buy a $350,000 home. You come up with a $30,000 down payment and you need a loan (mortgage) for the remaining $320,000. At an interest rate of 5% (which may be high, or low, depending on current interest rates when you are reading this book) and a 30 year term, the bank will be making over $238,000 in interest on that loan! The majority of that 'profit' is made in the first 10 years of the mortgage (amortization).

But don't feel too bad... at the end of that 30 year term, if property values are increasing even by just 3% a year, your $350,000 home will be worth $849,582!

That's an increase of almost $500,000 (half a million dollars) and all you needed to get started with was $30K! Nice...

There's really no other opportunity where you can borrow from a bank and ultimately make money on the deal.

And keep in mind that you can accomplish this with a small investment. You can buy a home with as little as 10% (or if you have really good credit, less) of the purchase price and the bank will finance the rest, and they'll finance it for decades, up to 25-30 years!

Why use your own money when you can use the bank's?

You can leverage their money to help grow and strengthen your own financial future.

At a Glance

- A mortgage is an opportunity to leverage the bank's money.

- You'll likely earn more in the long run than you pay back in interest and principal – appreciation increases the value of your home over time.

- It's a proven way to strengthen your financial future.

There is nothing like staying at home for real comfort.

Jane Austen

Have you ever seen a lender offer to loan more (regardless of credit) if the borrower is a home owner? That's because lenders LOVE to loan money to home owners, and that means that when YOU own your own home, you will have...

Reason #6
Borrowing Power!

When you buy a home, you gain a lot of financial credibility. Banks are much more willing to look at you as a more trustworthy person (or, in other words, a safer financial risk).

There's something about buying a home that makes you appear solid, responsible, and trustworthy to a bank.

This gives you more borrowing power.

When a bank considers you less of a risk, they're more willing to lend you money. And that in turn makes it a lot easier for you to:

- Buy a car

- Go back to school

- Start a business

- And more

You don't even have to have owned your home for long. And you don't need to have a lot of equity in your home to enjoy this kind of borrowing power.

The simple fact that you own a home shows the banks that you are more creditworthy, and that you're a good risk for loaning money to.

Keep in Mind...

This new-found borrowing power isn't something to take lightly. You don't want to use it to buy everything your heart desires. Instead, use your new borrowing power as a tool to increase your financial stability and worth. Leverage your borrowing power to get ahead in life instead of buying a bunch of sh...tuff that you don't really need (and probably won't even want anymore after a few months).

At a Glance

- By owning your own home you gain immediate borrowing power.

- If you are borrowing to purchase an asset instead of a liability, that's a very good idea.

- This borrowing power begins almost the first day you own your home.

- Use this ability to increase your financial stability and to get ahead.

Have you ever met an older person who owns their home, sells it, downsizes and has a LOT of money left over to improve their retirement? There are lots of them out there, and nowadays many retirees are using the equity in their homes to subsidize their retirement years.

Reason #7
Home Ownership Can Help You to Retire Comfortably

Depending on your age, retirement is something that you may not think about too often. However, the earlier you start thinking about it, the better off you'll be. Retirement can be super stressful as you get closer to those good old 'golden years.' And if you're not saving enough money, retirement can feel like a major crisis.

And let's be honest… pension plans and government retirement plans just don't cover it. Between the increasing demand on social services from the rise in baby-boomers who are ready to retire, and the hit that pensions took from the most recent stock market crash, you really do have to have a back-up plan if you want to retire comfortably.

Home Ownership Can be Your Retirement Back-Up Plan

Let's say that you're renting right now and not able to save much, if anything, for retirement. If you owned a home you could use the equity in your home and the appreciated value to help you during retirement.

If you're renting, nothing is happening with your money. Well... actually you are helping your landlord with his or her retirement plan, so something is happening with your money... it's just not happening for you!

But here's the good news! When you buy a home and you pay off your mortgage over time, by the time you're ready to retire you have a home that has tremendous equity and has appreciated in value.

That is money that you can use to:

- Invest

- Withdraw it slowly, over time

- Augment your income

---

*According to a well-known financial planner,
the average home owner has a net worth
EIGHTY TIMES (80x) greater than the average renter.*

Why wouldn't you want to retire comfortably?

And if you don't want to sell your home when you retire, you can STILL get access to most of that built up equity. How? With a...

Reverse Mortgage

A reverse mortgage is an option for many retirees. Here's how it works:

If you are a Canadian homeowner older than 55, you can get up to 50 percent of your home's value through a reverse mortgage. This means that you get money back from the equity you have in your home.

You are not required to make any mortgage payments and don't have to pay any interest or principal until you sell the home (or you pass away). The remainder of your mortgage is paid off from the proceeds of your home's sale.

This is just one way that your home can supplement your retirement income. This option isn't available to you if you rent, but if you are a home owner, it can provide tremendous comfort and financial security.

At a Glance

- Your home equity is a retirement backup plan.
- You can invest your equity and save more for retirement.
- You can withdraw your equity slowly over time and live off it.

- You can use your equity to supplement your income.
- A reverse mortgage is one option that allows you to enjoy a more secure retirement and financial future.

Let's face it... RENTING SUCKS! It's better than not having a roof over your head, but financially it really keeps you down.

Reason #8
The Alternative To Owning Your Own Home Is to Pay Rent, Which Does Nothing to Improve Your Finances

---

Admittedly, there are times when renting may be the better choice. If you're only going to be in a location for a short time – less than two years – then renting can be much easier. You're able to move quickly and you don't have to worry about selling a home.

That being said, even if you are in a community for a short time period, you can still make money from buying a home. It all depends on what kind of a deal you get on the place, and how much the area is appreciating in value. It's a decision that you'll have to weigh and decide what's best for you.

Setting Down Roots

When you find the place where you want to stay, or you know you'll be there for a few years, it's time to look at buying a home.

This isn't just because you want to feel part of a community and settle down. You may not actually be interested in that. Putting down roots isn't a priority for everyone.

However, most people do like to:

- Make the most of their money.

- Leverage their money.

- Grow their money by leveraging the OPM (other people's money).

When you own your own home, you are paying into your own future wealth. You are paying down your mortgage, increasing your equity, improving the quality of your home (and increasing its worth), benefitting from property appreciation and everything else.

It just makes sense to own! In most cases it certainly makes a lot more sense than renting.

You want your money to work for YOU, not for your landlord.

When you rent, all you are doing is paying for a roof over your head, and creating wealth for your landlord. You are paying down the landlord's mortgage, and helping him or her to benefit from property appreciation.

At a Glance

- Renting doesn't help you improve your financial situation.

- It doesn't give you any financial leverage.

- Owning a home is an investment and an opportunity to strengthen your financial future.

- Home ownership provides you with an opportunity to make your money work for you (instead of your landlord).

Owning a home is a keystone of wealth - both financial affluence and emotional security.

Suze Orman

We've been talking a lot about your house being a way to create long-term wealth for you through increasing equity. But did you know that you can also make money from your home today? That's because when you are a home owner.

Reason #9
Your Home Can Be a
Money Maker!

D id you know that you can actually get your home to give YOU a paycheck every month?

There are several ways that you can leverage home ownership and create income. Let's take a look at a few of those, because it's exciting to think about and if you begin taking steps now, you can realize the benefits of this additional income much sooner.

Rent Out a Room or Create a Rental Suite

There are homes that are perfectly suited to creating additional rental income for you. For example, you might look for a home that has a separate entrance into the basement, where you could build a small apartment complete with a kitchen and bathroom. The income from this suite could go a long way to covering your mortgage payment on the entire house!

You could rent out a room in your home to a friend or family member. You could also rent to a stranger, like a local university student. When you're looking for a home to fit this scenario you'll want to make sure that the home has enough bedrooms and bathrooms for the people who will be living there.

You can also look to buy a duplex; a home that's split into two smaller homes, and rent out one of the sides to a tenant while you live in the other.

The extra rental income can:

- Help you pay your bills.

- Go into a college fund if you have children.

- Be invested for additional income.

- Help you save for retirement.

- Be applied to your mortgage payment to bring down your monthly expenses.

These are just a couple of ideas for turning your home into a money maker.

You can also begin to create real estate assets for the future. Why don't YOU be the real estate investor / landlord?

If you've rented, then you know that the landlord has a pretty good deal. They rent to you, and you pay the monthly rent – which is usually a bit more than the cost of the mortgage.

For example, if the landlord pays $1,000 a month to the bank for the mortgage of the home you live in, they'll charge you $1,400 or more a month in rent. They are enjoying the appreciation and equity, and making some money on top of it.

You can become a real estate investor / landlord too.

Here's how that could work: Generally speaking, you will probably live in your home for a 4 or 5 years. After that you might feel like you've outgrown the home or you're ready to buy a different home.

Instead of doing the 'normal' thing and selling the house and buying another, why not KEEP the first one and turn it into a rental property?

You'll charge enough to cover your mortgage payment and probably more.

You'll enjoy the benefits of rental income, equity, and appreciation on your first home, and you can then also benefit from equity and appreciation on the home you buy and choose to live in.

Instead of BOGO (Buy One Get One Free) this is like BOKO (Buy One, Keep One Free).

And if you like that idea, how about this one...

Two Rental Units in One House!

Now imagine that you own a home that has a rental suite in the basement right now. You're able to gain rental income from that suite. And later, when you move out, you can then rent the upstairs separately. You now have two rental incomes to profit from –income from the upstairs unit that you were living in, plus the basement rental unit income you already had!

You rent both of these out. They more than cover the cost of your mortgage. You will probably even have money left over at the end of the day to help pay down the mortgage on your new house.

At a Glance

- You can make money from your home.

- You can rent out a room and reduce your mortgage expense, or make extra payments on your principal.

- You can rent out your home and become a landlord.

- Rental income can become part of your retirement savings, college savings, or you can invest it to make more money.

- Owning a home gives you the opportunity to turn your home into an income producer.

There is nothing more important than a good, safe, secure home.

Rosalynn Carter

O K, you are very familiar with the benefits of owning a home. That brings up the question "Now what?"

The benefits are apparent. They're tempting, wonderful, and you're ready to own a home. There's only one problem, you just can't afford it right now, or you don't quite qualify for a mortgage...

Right?

Actually, you might be surprised at what is possible when you really set your mind to it.

Perhaps there is an opportunity just waiting for you.

It's entirely possible that you could own a home sooner rather than later.

Let's take a look what's holding you back, and how you can get around that.

In the following section, we're going to explore the most common reasons why people don't qualify for a mortgage, and then share four different paths that you can take to overcome this challenge and become a home owner.

So You Don't Qualify For a Mortgage - What Are Your Options?

Qualifying for a mortgage can be tricky. Banks want to make sure that you are able to pay them back. They want to make sure you're a good credit risk.

Many people get turned down for a mortgage, and it can be emotionally devastating. Like I mentioned in the intro of this book, if you've filed for bankruptcy or have past credit challenges, then qualifying for a mortgage may seem like an impossible dream.

To get a mortgage you need a few key ingredients:

- You need a down payment.

- You need good credit, or at least acceptable credit.

- You need a decent debt-to-credit ratio – meaning you have more credit available to you than what you currently owe.

- You need a positive credit history.

- You need to be able to show consistent employment. (If you're self-employed then you may need a couple of years in business to prove you're a good credit risk.)

If you fall short in some of these areas, you might be shaking your head and feeling overwhelmed and stuck. There's just no way you can make the transition from home renter to home owner, or is there..?

Yes there is!

Let's take a look at a few of your options (and what I think is your BEST option).

Option #1
You Can Give Up and
Keep Renting

This is not a good option, but it is the default choice most people make. Why? Because renting is easy and predictable, right? Actually, renting isn't all that predictable at all!

Why Not? For a couple of reasons...

Your landlord can:

Raise Your Rent.

Let's say your rental agreement is up and your landlord decides that they should or can ask for more money. (In some provinces – Alberta, for example – they can raise it as much as they want) Now you have a surprise expense because your rent is significantly higher than it was before. Not much fun.

Kick You Out.

Your landlord can also decide to sell the house. If the new owner doesn't want the home to be a rental, this leaves you scrambling for a new place to live. It's not much fun and it doesn't feel fair. Though it's perfectly within your landlord's rights to do so.

So maybe renting isn't so easy and predictable after all.

And What About Your Debt?

If you have a lot of debt hanging over you, paying it off may be taking all of your cash. You may feel like not only are you never going to get caught up, but there's also no way that you can save any money for buying a home.

Sometimes it feels like the only way getting your own house would happen is if you win the lottery or a long lost relative leaves you their millions (and unfortunately neither of those possibilities is likely to happen).

So what can you do? You start to feel like you don't have any options and owning a home is never going to happen for you.

Let's look at another option…

Option #2
You Can Work To Fix Your Credit and Save Up for a Down Payment
(Also Known As "The D.I.Y. Method")

There are many ways that you can try to get your credit situation cleaned up and get ahead on your own. You can create your own credit repair strategy and savings plan. You can also find a debt reduction strategy online or in a book and try to follow it.

Both of those are viable options. The challenge to a pre-packaged or "do it yourself" ("DIY") debt repayment and savings plan is that you're all on your own. There's no one there to guide you through the process. You're like the Lone Ranger, and it's a little... lonely.

And chances are, if you have found yourself in a tough financial situation, you could use some help to get yourself out of it!

It's like an obese person trying to lose a hundred pounds

on their own, without any support or guidance. Or like trying to repair your car's engine yourself without any mechanical experience. Some people are able to make it happen. However, they're few and far between. It's incredibly difficult to do it on your own.

And...

Recent statistics suggest that the average family with a credit card owes more than $15,000!

It's almost impossible to climb out of that kind of debt on your own, and even more difficult to do it while trying to save money for a down payment on a home at the same time.

And that $15,000 number doesn't take into consideration the ridiculously high interest rates that most credit cards charge. It's why credit cards are considered the worst type of consumer debt. The interest rates can be up to 35 percent! That's highway robbery if you ask me!

So when you take that into account, it means that you're faced with seemingly insurmountable debt, and that debt continues to increase faster than you can pay it off.

That's another reason why a DIY strategy may be difficult to stick to without expert help, support, and guidance.

Plus, it also takes a LONG time. When you're working on your own to pay off your credit card debt and save money, it can take years and years for this to happen. You may experience tough times where you feel like you have to rely on your credit card, and that can set you back. And with high interest rates, it can take a while to pay off even a small amount of additional debt.

The Bottom Line - It's 'do-able', it's just not probable.

The bottom line is that you can come up with a plan to pay off debt all on your own, without help. And you can also create a plan to save money. If you do manage to pull it off, it won't be easy and it will take a long time.

However, if you are looking for a faster, and possibly easier, plan that allows you to live in your own home while you are doing it...

There are other options to consider...

Option #3
You Can Try To Do a
'Creative' Home Purchase Deal
on Your Own

Some people take matters into their own hands, find a house they like, and then try to get a little creative with their home purchase approach.

Sometimes it's possible to agree with a property seller and do a "creative deal."

What's a "creative real estate deal?"

Example #1: VTB (Vendor Take Back)

Together you could work out a deal where the seller or owner of the home finances it for you. So instead of going to the bank for a loan, you'd buy the property and owe the money to the existing home owner. It's often referred to as vendor financing or a vendor "take back" mortgage.

The benefit of this approach is that you don't have to qualify for a bank loan. You don't have to go through the approval process or even a credit check. That can be a huge benefit for people who have bad credit or who have been turned down by the bank before.

However, as good as this might sound…

There are a few problems with this approach.

The first is that it's extremely difficult to find a home owner who is both willing and able to do this type of agreement. They have to own the home outright in order to be able to do this – meaning they don't have a mortgage on the home.

They also need to be willing to take a risk on you and your ability to pay them back. This means that they have to like you… a LOT!

Plus they have to want to sell the home to you this way, and get paid out slowly, over time. Most people would much rather get CASH for their property and deal with home buyers the traditional way. It gives them more leverage and power over their money.

Chances are, you are going to have to look at a LOT of properties and make an awful lot of offers before you find a home seller who is even remotely interested in discussing the idea. And forget about trying to do this through a realtor! There is NO WAY a realtor is going to work with you (because they want to get paid a commission up front… and that won't happen fast enough for them if their client does an owner-financing deal).

This means that you are going to have to scour the classified ads for FSBO (For Sale By Owner) properties, and make a lot of phone calls before you get someone who is interested. Then you will have to visit the home, create a bit of a 'relationship' with the seller (so they get to like you and are willing to do a VTB). Then you will have to get the paperwork done up with a lawyer to make sure that you and the seller are protected and that the deal is very clear and understandable.

And here's another challenge... the property itself. There is probably some kind of challenge with the property itself in order for the seller to be willing to finance you for it. That means you might have to come up with a lot of money down the road to fix whatever is wrong with it.

Plus, you will likely have to 'make do' with the property. This property would probably NOT be your first choice for a home if you had the money and credit to be picky.

And finally, you usually need to have quite a bit of cash up front for the seller to feel comfortable selling you the home this way. And you will likely pay much higher interest rates to the home owner than you would to the bank, so it can be more expensive.

Okay, getting a seller to finance you to buy their house is an option for you. It's a lot easier said than done, but it is possible.

However there is another way that might just be the best of all worlds for you, and that is option number 4...

Option #4
You Can "Rent to Own" Your Dream Home NOW!

P urchasing a nice home through a Rent to Own is a very real possibility. It's a proven way to help you improve your credit, and save up your down payment while you're living in the home you're eventually going to buy.

Rent to Own makes a lot of sense if you:

- Are tired of watching your money disappear.

- Want to leverage your money and gain equity from your home.

- Feel you're ready to set down roots.

- Want to benefit from increased borrowing power.

- Want a forced savings account (that you can use for emergencies).

- Are considering turning your home into an income producer now or in the future.

Then rent to own can be your ideal solution.

Let's take a look at the two different types of rent to own that are available to you... Traditional and Client First.

*He is happiest, be he king or peasant,
who finds peace in his home.*

Johann Wolfgang von Goethe

The Two Main Types of Rent to Own

The Traditional Rent-to-Own Approach

Traditional rent to own may be something that you're already familiar with.

In this situation the landlord has decided that they want to sell their property. It might be because they are ready to get out of the rental business, or maybe they just want to retire. Unfortunately, it can also happen when the house is difficult to rent or getting too costly to maintain.

It's a challenging property for the landlord for one reason or another, so they decide to use a rent-to-own strategy to get rid of it. Keep in mind that most times the landlord may have already tried to sell the home, 'the normal way' on their own or with a realtor. The home may need too much work or it may have an unusual layout so a normal sale is difficult.

Doing a rent to own offers them a way of getting rid of their unwanted property, and it gives renters an opportunity to own a home.

It's a Bottom Up Approach

Generally speaking, when a homebuyer begins looking for a home to purchase they're able to look at a number of properties in their price range and make an offer on the one they like the best.

With a traditional rent to own, you only have one house to look at... one choice. The owner says, "here's the home, take it or leave it."

That is your only choice.

If you decide to take it, then you have to work out a rent-to-own arrangement with them.

Generally, these traditional rent-to-own agreements are made up of two agreements:

1. A standard lease agreement, and

2. An option to purchase.

These may be combined into one document or kept as two separate documents.

It usually works like this....

Together you and your landlord work out an agreement. They agree that you can buy the home from them at a future date, and that a part of your monthly rent payments are going to be put towards buying the property (either towards the down payment, or as a reduction in the final sales price). These are typically called 'rental credits.' The "option to purchase" or "agreement to purchase" gives you the option or the right to buy the property within a specified period of time and for a specific price.

The landlord will typically want an upfront fee for the option, and that may or may not apply towards the final price or the down payment as well.

Here's the kicker...

You are usually responsible for all of the repairs and maintenance of the property under this type of agreement. That means, for example, if the roof needs to be replaced, the hot water tanks blows, or the basement floods – that expense falls on your shoulders.

And...

If you decide that you don't want to purchase the home, you are usually not refunded the option fee or any of your rental credits. All of that money that you paid over and above your typical rent payment is lost.

Having a weak (or even non-existent) contract is a challenge with these kinds of deals – the paperwork is often unprofessional, or very one-sided (in the favor of the landlord).

Unfortunately, traditional rent-to-own deals fall through more often than not, and as the tenant-buyer, you're usually left without any recourse.

If you choose this to do a 'traditional' rent to own, and it can work in some circumstances, then it's very important to make sure that your agreement is solid, that you're prepared to handle the home repairs during this time, and that you are completely sure that you really want to buy that particular home.

There's a lot at stake with this type of rent-to-own deal. Make sure that you get your own legal counsel before signing the contract or paying any money towards the property. Now, what if there was a BETTER WAY to get into your home through rent-to-own? What if there was a way where YOU could CHOOSE the home you want to live in, and then rent-to-own it while you automatically save up your down payment and someone helps you to get your credit in order so that you can qualify for a mortgage to buy the home in a few short years?

There is! And that's exactly what we are going to look at next.

The Client First
Rent-to-Own Method

This rent-to-own approach puts you first! You're the client and the process is quite different – because it puts your needs and preferences FIRST.

First you will start by sitting with the rent-to-own professional ("R2O Pro" for short) and look at how much of a home you can afford, as well as what kind of house you are looking for. Once you have that figured out, you get to go house shopping! You will be working with a realtor, and you get to enjoy the process of shopping for your future home.

You choose a home that you like, and the R2O Pro that you're working with handles the negotiation process, and then actually purchases the home for you!

This allows you to move into your 'dream home' and live in it while giving you the time you need to get qualified to purchase the home AND accumulate your down payment in installments!

It doesn't get much better than that! You pick the house,

the R2O Pro buys it for you, and you get to live in it while having the time you need to be able to buy it!

Once you're in your dream home you pay rent plus a little more that will be put toward your down payment. The extra on top of your rent is called a rental credit.

You and the R2O Pro will agree on a specific amount of time that your rent-to-own term will be, the rental amount, the amount you will accumulate towards your down payment, and the final price you will be paying for the house. All of this will be done up front.

Then, at the end of the term, you will have enough money accumulated to make the down payment, and your credit will be acceptable to a lender, and at that time, the R2O Pro sells you the home!

It's now 100% YOURS!

You own the home.

Getting Started with Client First Rent to Own

There's a simple and relatively straightforward process to a client first rent to own. We'll take an in depth look at each step in a few pages, but for now let's simply outline them so you know what to expect.

1 – Apply to a Legitimate Rent-to-Own Program with an Experienced R2O Pro

There are a few criteria that you have to meet in order to be considered for this type of program. Usually this involves filling out an application, and giving some background information. All of this is completely confidential.

2 – Search for a Home

Based on your price range you'll work with a real estate agent to find a home that meets your needs. Keep in mind that there may be some basic parameters set by the rent-to-own organization as well.

They have your best interests in mind and want to make sure that you're buying a home that is in good condition, that you can afford, and that will likely appreciate over time.

3 – You Choose Your Home

Once you choose a few homes that you're interested in, they get to work for you. They'll negotiate with the seller and buy the home for you.

4 –You Move into Your New Home

You move into your new home and begin the process of renting to own. After a few years of renting and accumulating credits towards your down payment, you'll transition to a traditional mortgage. You'll pay rent as you live in your home and after a few years, you'll own the home. It's yours!

5 – You Qualify for a Mortgage

After a few years of saving and repairing your credit, you'll be where you need in order to apply for a mortgage. You'll close on the house and transition from being renter to being the owner.

You're now able to begin benefitting from home ownership. Remember that means...

- Equity

- Emergency savings

- Secure retirement

- Income potential

- Appreciation

- And more

Next, we'll take a look at how to achieve rent-to-own success, and walk through the steps you'll take to become a home owner sooner rather than later with rent-to-own!

*The thrill of coming home
has never changed.*

Guy Pearce

8 Steps to Rent-to-Own Success

The client first rent-to-own process puts you, the client, first. It doesn't matter where you're coming from. If you meet the basic criteria of the R2O Pro you are working with, you can be living in a home that you choose within a few short months, and be on your way to full-fledged ownership in just a few short years!

Now the "Criteria" aspect of the process may have you a bit worried. You might wonder what makes someone a good rent-to-own applicant.

We already understand that you're in the rent-to-own market because you're probably facing some financial challenges.

That's okay.

During the application process we want to know:

- That you're willing to work hard, with our help, to improve your credit.

- That you make enough money to afford to rent to own a nice home for you and your family.

- And that you have realistic expectations.

Let's take a look at what it means to have realistic expectations first, and then we'll talk about the steps in the rent-to-own process. Understanding what to expect can help you be prepared for the path to becoming a home owner through rent-to-own.

Step #1
Having Realistic Expectations

What does it mean to have realistic expectations when buying a rent-to-own property? Realistic expectations mean that you have a firm grasp about where you are starting from right now, what you're able to afford, and that you're realistic about the rent-to-own buying process. Let's explore each of these expectations in more detail.

Realistic About How Much You Can Afford

We all want to live in a home that costs much more than we can afford. Who wouldn't want to live in a multi-million dollar mansion? Sometimes those dreams can cause people to get carried away. When it comes to home ownership, keep in mind that you are either just starting out (or starting over), and that means that your first home may be a bit different than what you see on television – and perhaps even what you believe you can afford.

The price of homes can catch people by surprise.

If you've been paying rent for years and you're just now starting to look at buying, you may be surprised at the cost of homes in your desired area or community. That isn't to say that you can't find a wonderful home in your price range. You probably can.

It's simply important that your home wish list matches your income. You'll waste your time if you spend it looking for a house that you cannot afford. Maximize your time and your money and work with your R2O Pro to find a good home in your price range.

If you're smart with your money, you may be living in that multi-million dollar mansion someday soon.

As a general guideline, your monthly mortgage payment, including principal, interest, real estate taxes and homeowners insurance, should not exceed 30 percent of your gross monthly income (the total amount you and your spouse make BEFORE taxes).

To calculate your housing expense ratio, multiply your annual salary by 0.30, then divide by 12 (months).

For example, if you make $70,000 annually then your rent/mortgage payment shouldn't exceed $1,750 a month.

$$\$70,000 * 0.30 = \$21,000$$

$$\$21,000 / 12 = \$1,750$$

Realistic About the Time Frame

Once you are in the home, it is easy to think that it's already yours... but it isn't yours quite yet. You still need time to:

a. Get your credit to a level where you can qualify for a mortgage, and...

b. Accumulate enough credits towards your down payment to be able to actually buy the property.

Everybody would love to do this ASAP, but the reality is that it usually takes around 3 years to make this all come together.

In the big picture, 3 years isn't a very long time to be able to buy a home... especially if you are already living in it all that time anyway!

So we know that you are excited to have a home to call your own sooner rather than later. It's also important to clearly understand how long it takes to repair your credit situation, as well as how much you will need to accumulate for a down payment. This is why having realistic time expectations are so important.

Be Realistic About How Much Your Monthly Rent Will Be.

Here's the bottom line: Rent-to-Own rent is HIGHER than normal rent.

It's higher for two reasons.

1. In a rent-to-own deal, a portion of your monthly rent is credited back to you as a rental credit, and...

2. The R2O Pro you are working with is doing this as a business, and deserves to make a profit for doing so.

When it comes to your monthly rental credits, it goes back to the concept of a forced savings plan. This monthly payment helps you save for your down payment, in installments.

Each month you'll pay your rent and a portion of that will be credited toward your down payment. Typically about 20 percent of your total rent is applied toward your down payment each month. You'll chip away at that down payment and in a few years you'll have it and can transition out of the rental deal and into ownership.

So that means that your R2O rent for that home is probably 15-20% more than you would pay just to 'rent' a similar property.

A Sample Breakdown of Your Monthly Rent to Own Payment

Rent – $1600

Rental Credit – $400 (25%)

Total Monthly Payment – $2000

And let's take a look at reason #2. That your R2O Pro is doing this as a business, and deserves to make some profit for helping you.

It's important to remember exactly how much your R2O Pro is helping you here. Who else do you know who will come up with tens of thousands of dollars to buy you a house that you choose?

It actually costs your R2O Pro 20% of the purchase price of the property as a down payment, PLUS closing costs etc. So this is no small investment for them.

A portion of their 'profit' on these deals comes from the difference between what you pay for rent (and rental credits) and what their total expenses are on the property.

So if you want rock-bottom rent prices, you are going to have to keep renting. Rent-to-own won't work that way.

Your R2O professional is charging you higher than market rent in order to help you save up your down payment in installments through rental credits. Plus, the R2O Pro needs to see some return on their investment during the deal. Fair is fair.

Realistic Expectations – Some Skin in the Game

Finally, you want to be committed to the process and have what we call, "skin in the game." This is a term coined by Warren Buffet and it means that you're investing some of your own money into the deal.

When it comes to a rent-to-own agreement, this means that you have some form of an up front fee or 'option fee' to get the process started. The typical up front option fee that a rent-to-own deal requires is 4 or 5% of the value of the home.

For example, if you're looking at homes in the $300,000 range, then five percent of that is $15,000. This is a non-refundable option fee and it will be applied toward your down payment when you purchase the home.

It's your "skin" so to speak, and a commitment to the agreement. If you don't purchase the home, you don't get that money back. However, when you do follow through, keep your agreement and purchase the home, then you already have 5% of your down payment taken care of!

Cost of home - $300,000
Non-refundable down payment option - $15,000
Total down payment needed (10%) - $30,000

Now that you have some realistic and clear expectations, the next step is to fill out the online application. This process takes just a few minutes and it's 100% confidential, quick, easy, and painless.

Step #2
Fill Out the Rent-to-Own Application

This is the easy part, and it can be one of the most exciting moments of your life! It's the moment where you start to take control over your life and your money, and you begin on your journey to home ownership.

It's a simple, online application and you don't need any financial information right now, nor do you need tax info or a stress ball to help you cope with the process. Mostly it's as simple as answering yes or no to some very basic questions.

(Check out our website and contact information on the back cover, and fill out your no-obligation application today.)

In addition to the normal contact information, here is a sample of what we will be asking you:

- How long have you worked at your present job?

- What is your combined household income?

- How much do you have in savings?

- What do you pay in rent now?

- How much of a monthly payment can you afford?

- Have you ever filed for bankruptcy?

- If yes, did you file alone or with your spouse?

- If yes, was it discharged?

- If yes, when?

- What area(s) would you like your new house to be in?

- What kind of home would you like?

- What price range of home do you think will fit into your budget?

As you can see, those are easy questions to answer, and the application process is quick and painless.

(If you would like to work with us, please check the back cover of this book, visit out our website and fill out our private, no-obligation application today.)

Let's take a look at the next step. What happens after you've filled out your rent-to-own application?

Step #3
Have a Meeting in Person

Once your application has been reviewed, you'll be contacted to set up a meeting. At the meeting you'll have the opportunity to discuss your wants, needs, and goals for home ownership.

You'll talk with an R2O Pro about what you're looking for in a home. This is where you can discuss the finer details of your future home, including:

- How many bedrooms your home should have.

- The number of bathrooms you'd prefer.

- The size of the home.

- The style of home. For example, you may prefer a two-story over a ranch style home.

- How large of a yard you'd like.

- As well as your ideal location, school district and more.

This gives your R2O Pro the information they need so that they can guide the real estate agent to show you the homes that fit your needs.

You'll also discuss the financial aspects of your present situation. And although it may seem a little scary or embarrassing to discuss your finances with someone, it's important to keep in mind that:

This program is specifically designed for people who are not quite able to qualify for a traditional mortgage right now, but who are looking for a way to own their home instead of continuing to pay rent month after month after month.

Your lack of credit or not-so-great credit score are factors relating to your past, and not necessarily part of your current financial situation nor your future. Your past is less important to us than your future.

If you have steady income, your R2O Pro will work with you to create a rent-to-own plan that meets your financial needs and goals.

(If you would like to work with us, please check the back cover of this book, visit out our website and we'll get back to you shortly.)

Your one-on-one meeting will help outline your financial and home ownership goals, so that you can move onto the next step, which is the step you've been waiting for!

Step #4
House Shopping!
Choose Your New Home!

Have you ever spent time shopping for a home? Once you've worked with your R2O Pro and you've established your needs in a home (including size, number of bedrooms, and location), and you've worked out the financial details, it's time to go shopping!

Our friendly real estate agent will show you a number of homes that match your criteria.

You'll get to tour the homes and ask questions – it's just like a traditional home buying process.

You might be surprised how tiring it can be when you shop for a home. Viewing a number of homes is emotional. You'll be excited and thrilled while also potentially overwhelmed at the same time.

Your R2O Pro and the real estate agent may have recommendations to help you track what you like about each home. Consider bringing a notebook and pen with you so you can write down key information. You may also want to bring a camera or your smartphone with you so that you can remember the homes inside and out.

Once you've viewed the homes in your area that fit your needs, you'll have the opportunity to pick one or more that you're interested in.

Then Your R2O Pro Gets to Work for You

After you've made your decision, your R2O Pro will go to work for you and begin the negotiation and home buying process.

Once the deal is done, you're on your way to owning your home. In approximately three years you'll have your down payment accumulated, your credit problems will be in the past and you'll be able to qualify for a mortgage (if you follow the plan).

Now that we've looked at the 'fun' part of this Client-First Rent-to-Own program, you may be ready to jump in right away. That's great, but there's one step that you must take first...

Step #5
Cover Your Ass...ets

D oing a rent-to-own deal means that, in a sense, you're putting your future into someone else's hands. You're trusting experts to help you get from where you are now – a renter with credit challenges – to an owner who can qualify for a mortgage.

You want to make sure that you trust the right people.

Make Sure You are Working with a Reputable Company

The first step to covering your assets and protecting yourself is to make sure that the company you're working with, or considering working with, has a good reputation.

You can learn a bit about a company by searching online for reviews, testimonials, and feedback about them.

Unfortunately there are a good number of so-called rent-to-own operators that are unprofessional. They don't use proper channels. They don't have good paperwork or contracts (in fact, some don't have contracts at all).

Not having a good contract can spell disaster for you! Would you buy a home and give someone your money on just a handshake?

You want to make sure...

- You are getting documentation to show where all of the money is going.

- You are able to look at the contract and paperwork prior to getting into the deal.

- You are signing the contract with a reputable R2O Pro.

- You have the opportunity to have your own lawyer look over the contract and the paperwork.

- You have a clear understanding exactly how the whole process works.

- You know what your legal rights and responsibilities are.

Too many people get burned when they make deals with unprofessional organizations.

Don't let this be you.

Step #6
Paying In Your Down Payment in Installments

You've chosen your home and you've made certain that the agreements you're signing and the company you're working with are reputable and working for your best interests. You know they're professional and you trust them to represent you.

The next step, once they've negotiated the home price, is to move in and begin accumulating your down payment in installments.

Rental Credits

As we mentioned earlier, with the rent-to-own process a portion of your total monthly payment is called a rental credit. This rental credit is what you're saving for your down payment to eventually buy the home from your R2O Pro.

Here's an example of how it works.

Let's say that your total monthly payment is $2000.

$400 to $500 (20 percent to 25 percent) of that payment is applied toward your rental credits.

That means that you're paying $1500 to $1600 in monthly rent and the rest is being applied towards your down payment, so that in a few years you'll be able to qualify for a mortgage.

It's part of the process of qualifying for financing. Banks want you to have a healthy down payment before they give you a mortgage (and nowadays they want to see 10% down from people who have had previous credit challenges).

Let's take a look at that step next, because being able to buy the home in a couple of years is the ultimate goal, right? You're renting to own while you work to overcome your credit challenges and save for your down payment.

Step #7
Qualifying for Financing

One of the benefits of rent to own is that it can be a BIG part of your credit repair process. Instead of paying rent and flushing those payments to the landlord down the tube, with rent-to-own you are actually putting some of that money aside towards your down payment. This helps you approach the banks and qualify for financing.

However, that's not the only challenge that you may be facing.

You may need to establish credit in the first place.

Or

You may have credit debt that you need to pay off.

Earlier we talked about what the bank needs in order to give you a home loan.

To get a mortgage you need a few key ingredients:

- You need a down payment – you will have that covered with the rental credits and up-front option fee.

- You need good credit, or at least acceptable credit.

- You need a decent debt-to-credit ratio – meaning you have more credit available to you than you owe. In other words, your credit cards cannot be maxed out.

- You need a positive credit history (usually for 2-3 years).

Part of the rent-to-own process with a good R2O Pro is to help you create a comprehensive credit repair plan. It's part of your deal. The company you're working with should want to make sure that you are able to get your credit where you need it, so that when the time is right, when you have your down payment ready to go, you WILL qualify for your mortgage and be able to buy the house from them.

In addition to creating a credit repair plan with you, a good R2O Pro will support you throughout the process. They will follow up, offer guidance, and help along the way.

What to Expect from the Credit Repair Process

During the credit repair process your R2O Pro should work with you to assess where you are right now, so they can create a realistic plan with you to repair your credit and get your financing. This is the 'start up' plan.

Then you need to have a follow-up plan, which should ideally include quarterly visits and updates. Your R2O Pro will meet with you to see where you are in the process. Are you on track or are you facing additional challenges?

Your R2O Pro may do this themselves, or they may refer you to a qualified credit coach instead.

In either case, they'll work with you to help solve those problems if they come up, and they'll strive to help you avoid any future credit repair problems that might slow down your big goal of buying the home.

Most rent-to-own organizations do not offer this level of service and support.

It's up to you to find a Client-First Rent-to-Own company that has your back.

Whoever you work with, make sure you take the time to ask if they provide any assistance with their credit repair process. If they don't, you may want to consider continuing your search.

When Everything Comes Together

If everything works properly, then at the end of the process you should have enough money built up to cover your down payment and your closing costs.

The goal is to have between 10 and 12 percent of the final purchase price paid in prior to closing.

You'll work with your R2O Pro to find an option that works for you as you save toward your new home.

Step #8
Buying the Home!

O K, now we're getting to the really exciting stuff! 24 to 36 months have flown by, and through your initial option fee and rental credits, you've saved 10 to 12 percent of the cost of your home. Fantastic! You have enough to make a down payment and to cover your closing costs!

You have also followed the credit repair plan and your credit is in good shape, and you've qualified for a mortgage.

Congratulations!

You're about to become a true blue home owner.

You will work closely with your R2O Pro, a mortgage broker and a lawyer to close the deal. This process will usually take 45-60 days (the last couple of months of your rent-to-own term).

You've worked hard to make it to this point and it's time to celebrate. Host a party, buy new furniture or enjoy a nice meal with your family.

You're now on your way to the equity home ownership provides and all of the leverage, power, and benefits that go with it. Those benefits include, but aren't limited to:

- Appreciation – your home appreciates in value over the long term.

- The pride and satisfaction of home ownership.

- Freedom to create the home you want – no need to follow the landlord's rules.

- You can borrow against your home equity in an emergency.

- The equity portion of your mortgage payment is a form of automatic savings.

- Increased borrowing power.

- Home ownership can help you to retire comfortably.

- Your home can be an income producer.

Next, let's talk about some of the common mistakes and challenges that can occur during the rent-to-own process and, most importantly, how to avoid them so you can have a productive and enjoyable transition to home ownership.

*A comfortable house is
a great source of happiness.*

Sydney Smith

Common Rent to Own Mistakes, Challenges, and Traps (And How to Avoid Them)

Rent to Own Mistake #1: Scumbag Landlords

Rent to own can be a dream come true for many families who have credit challenges and don't currently qualify for a mortgage.

However...

It can also be a nightmare if you end up working with an unscrupulous landlord who preys on families.

Here's how they work...

These scumbags prey on unsuspecting renters by promising them the world, in the form of a beautiful house, and then setting them up to fail.

They get as much money up front as they can

They charge you a ridiculous amount of rent.

They tell you that the upfront money and a part of the rent will be credited to you to help buy the house

With the exception of the large cash outlay that's required, this sounds pretty straightforward, right?

Here's where it gets sleazy.

There's some fine print that they don't want you to read and they sure as heck aren't going to tell you about.

The "fine print"....

If you are a day late, just one day late, with the rent then the agreement is void, they start eviction proceedings and you forfeit everything.

You lose your initial option fee.

You lose everything that you've invested into the home and all that exorbitant rent you've been paying… it's gone.

There's another way these scum-bags take your money.

They create impossible scenarios where the term is too short for you to get your credit fixed. These are usually 6, 12 or 18 month terms.

As you know, it takes time to repair credit. And if your credit isn't in good shape you won't qualify for the mortgage, so guess what happens when you don't qualify?

They kick you out.

They can also put you in a home that is too expensive for your income level so the bank is almost certain to deny you financing. And again, when that happens, they kick you out. You lose everything.

These scumbags really don't care. All they wanted was your money, and now that you're out of the home they'll turn around and do the same thing to someone else.

It's an understatement to say that they give the rent-to-own business a bad reputation.

Don't let this happen to you! Learn how to identify a rent to own scumbag.

How to Identify a Rent to Own Scumbag

- Pay attention to the house. These jerks rent-to-own the same house repeatedly. One victim after another is funneled through the same property. If a house is repeatedly offered as rent to own, it's a bad sign.

- Landlord doesn't want you to review the deal with your lawyer.

- Landlord doesn't ask many questions about your financial situation – they don't really care.

- Landlord is vague about details of the deal and "what-if" scenarios.

- Landlord pushes through the process and doesn't give you time to look closely at the agreement or to review the paperwork.

- The landlord doesn't have professional rent-to-own paperwork, and is relying on a standard rental agreement and a 'handshake' for the rest.

How to Avoid Making this Mistake:

- Always have a lawyer review the deal with you.

- Make sure there is an overview agreement explaining how the whole deal works.

- Make sure there is a formal lease, along with an agreement to purchase or option to purchase agreement.

- Beware if the person does not ask about your financial

situation and go over your plan to get qualified for a mortgage.

- Work with a professional rent-to-own company that has a good reputation.

(If you would like to work with us, please check the back cover of this book, visit out our website and we'll get back to you shortly.)

Rent to Own Mistake #2: Agreeing to Buy an Inadequate House

Most traditional rent-to-own opportunities are "house specific". This means that a landlord or Investor has a specific house that they want to sell as a rent to own, and that is the only option they have available for you.

Most often these properties are sold this way because they are not sellable in the normal way. Perhaps they:

- Are outdated and need a lot of refurbishing.

- Have a strange lay-out. For example, you have to walk through a bedroom to get to the only bathroom.

- Have a bad history. For example, the house may have been part of a crime scene or a meth lab.

- Have some other problem that makes it difficult to sell on the open market.

- Have an owner who wants to get a higher than normal market price for the house.

These homes often seem like good deals initially.

However, after some time in the home you may realize your mistake. When this happens there are one of two approaches you might take.

You might back out of the deal, and when this happens lose all your money. You walk away with nothing.

Or

You stick with the deal and hope to sell the house once you own it so that you can find a home that's more suitable. Chances are you'll take a loss because the house has problems.

How to Avoid Making This Mistake:

Work with a professional rent-to-own company (R2O Pro) that actually lets you choose the home that you live in. They shouldn't just be giving you one choice and saying 'take it or leave it.'

A client-first approach lets <u>you</u> select the ideal home that fits your needs and your budget. You can pick from any home that is on the market that meets your and the R2O Pro's criteria and price range. The rent-to-own company then buys the home for you, and you rent to own it from them until you're ready to buy it.

Don't let someone else choose your dream home. When you select the home you want in the first place, you will be happy to be in it for years to come!

(If you would like to work with us, please check the back cover of this book, visit out our website and we'll get back to you shortly.)

Rent to Own Mistake #3: Unprofessional and Incomplete Paperwork

Having the correct paperwork in order is vital to a successful rent-to-own home purchase. If you don't have the right paperwork, you can lose the deal. All your hard work will go down the drain and you'll have to start over.

Here's What You Need

You need to have the proper lease agreement, an option to buy, and a contract to purchase all in place in order for the deal to be legally binding. Without the proper agreements in place you won't be able to seal the deal, so to speak. You won't be able to follow through on the rent-to-own agreement and own the home.

The Wording Matters

If the wording in the agreement is not written properly,

there's a good chance that the bank won't recognize your investment. The deposit you made and the rental credits that you've accumulated will not be recognized.

There's no way a bank is going to approve your financing and give you a mortgage without a down payment. Remember that all of your rental credits and your deposit <u>are</u> your down payment. They must be accounted for properly and clearly in the contracts and documentation.

Otherwise you risk losing the deal and your money.

How to Avoid Making This Mistake:

The first and best way to avoid this mistake is to only work with reputable rent-to-own companies – R2O Pros. Don't work with inexperienced individuals, questionable rent-to-own operators, or scumbag landlords.

However, if you do decide to go forward with a private deal, make sure that you have a highly qualified real estate lawyer create the documents for you.

Then have your mortgage broker review them to be sure their lenders will accept them as proof of the money you have paid in.

Both of these steps, hiring a lawyer and paying a mortgage broker for their time, will cost you money.

A better option is to work with a R2O Pro that puts you, the client, first and has your success as their ultimate goal.

(If you would like to work with us, please check the back cover of this book, visit out our website and we'll get back to you shortly.)

Rent to Own Mistake #4: A Rushed Deal

I t's completely understandable and natural that you want your rent-to-own deal to be as short as possible. The sooner you get through it, the sooner you'll be a home owner.

Unfortunately, if you don't give yourself enough time, it can end in disaster.

Why?

First of all, you need enough time to get your credit to a place where a bank will give you a mortgage. Depending on your current situation, that usually takes two to three years.

Secondly, you also need to make sure that you have enough money put aside (or accumulated) for your down payment. Nowadays, the big banks are looking for people with 'less than perfect' credit to have a 10% down payment in order to get financing. In a rent-to-own deal, your down payment comes from your initial option fee, along with the monthly rental credits you get every month of the term. That process takes time.

Your rental credits come from your monthly rent. If you

rush the deal, you won't have enough rental credits, and then the rest of your down payment will have to come from your pocket.

So the beauty of a well-designed rent-to-own deal is this: you can live in your dream house while having all the time you need to improve your credit AND accumulate your down payment over time.

How to Avoid Making This Mistake:

The best way to avoid a rushed R2O deal is to work with a R2O Pro and their team, providing credit coaching as part of your rent-to-own deal and part of their services.

If you do decide that a private rent-to-own deal is the way to go, make sure that you get a complete "financial checkup" beforehand. You can sit down with a credit repair specialist or book an appointment with a mortgage broker to see where you stand.

Ask them to provide you with a detailed action plan that has a realistic time frame and then get to work improving your finances so that you can qualify for a mortgage.

Keep in mind that with a R2O Pro working with you, you can save for a down payment and repair your credit at the same time. You won't be going it alone. You not only receive a comprehensive action plan, you get regular checkups and support with the process.

(If you would like to work with us, please check the back cover of this book, visit out our website and we'll get back to you shortly.)

Rent to Own Mistake #5: Working with Mediocre Rent-to-Own Companies or Inexperienced Real Estate Investors

O ccasionally you'll come across a rent-to-own situation where the people involved generally have good intentions – they just don't know what they're doing.

There are many people who want to be part of the rent-to-own industry. Unfortunately, they don't have the knowledge, experience, team or finances required to do a good job for you. They're often unable to complete the deal as originally planned, and that very well may leave you with nothing.

Your dreams of owning a home are too important and, good intentions or not, if their inexperience costs you thousands of dollars, years of wasted time, and the house of your dreams, then it's not worth it.

Make sure that you're dealing with an experienced and highly professional rent-to-own company and R2O Pro. Let's take a look at a few signs of trouble, and then we'll look at how you can avoid these well-intentioned but inexperienced folks.

Red Flags:

- Small time real estate investors with little or no experience.

- If they only do real estate investing "part-time."

- A Jack of All Trades. Some investors try to offer many different types of services, including rent to own. You want a specialist, not an occasional rent-to-own investor.

- They only want to put you into one specific home they already have.

- They don't have many options for you. In some cases they may not have any options. They're just not prepared.

How to Avoid Making this Mistake:

- Look at the history of the rent-to-own company. Have they been in business for a while? Are they professionals? Have they had training? Are they part of a professional industry association?

- Do they specialize in the communities where you're looking for a home?

- What is their background? What education and experience does the staff have?

- What do others have to say about them? Do they have a good rating and good reviews? Do they appear professional, organized, and ready to help you become a home owner?

- Do they specialize in rent to own?

Shop around for the best rent-to-own company and R2O Pro you can find. Look for a company that specializes in rent to own – one that has an outstanding team and a solid presence in the community.

(If you would like to work with us, please check the back cover of this book, visit out our website and we'll get back to you shortly.)

Rent to Own Mistake #6: Not Understanding Your Current Situation and Where You Are Starting From

t's so easy to become focused on the future, and owning a home, that you forget to take stock of your present circumstances.

It's important to have a good understanding of your current credit situation. Not only do you need to know your present situation, it's a good idea to understand how your present financial situation will impact your rent-to-own process.

Your credit situation needs to be fixable in a specific time frame.

For most, it's not enough just to have a deposit and to pay your rent. You also need to be able to repair your credit while you're paying rent so that you can actually buy and own the home within a few years.

The problem with private rent-to-own deals, or deals with

an inferior rent-to-own business, is that they don't help you with your credit repair. It's left up to you to know and understand your credit score, how long it will take to repair it and how to fix it.

They are leaving you on your own.

That Doesn't Mean Your Situation Has To Be Perfect

Even if you are currently going through bankruptcy, you can still do a good rent-to-own deal. However, you need to know exactly how long it will take before you are "back on track."

When will the bank feel comfortable loaning you money? What do you have to do to become a safe investment in the bank's eyes? Also, what do you have to do to stay in their good graces?

Why Is This Information So Important?

If you don't know exactly where you are starting from, you can't accurately predict when you'll be able to qualify for a mortgage. If that's the case, you'll be setting yourself up for failure because you won't be able to qualify for a mortgage and buy the house when you agreed to.

How to Avoid Making This Mistake:

The first step is to get your credit score and a complete credit report from Equifax.ca. Review the report with a professional credit repair specialist to see exactly where you are.

You can also work with a quality rent-to-own company that does all of this with you.

They'll grab your credit report and score for you (or show you how to get it yourself).

They'll walk you through the report and show you what the information means and how it impacts your rent-to-own process.

They'll come up with a comprehensive credit repair plan specifically designed for you and your unique situation. The rent-to-own term and payment plan will be designed to fit your needs so that when the time is right, you'll be able to qualify for a mortgage.

(Check out our website and contact information on the back cover, and fill out your no-obligation application today.)

Rent to Own Mistake #7: Working With an Out of Town Rent-to-Own Company

Rent-to-own companies can be based anywhere. With today's technology they can negotiate, have meetings, and set everything up for a rent-to-own deal over the phone or by email.

It's also quite possible that a rent-to-own company on the other side of the country could have a part-time employee in your area. Generally speaking, that may seem like it's good enough. Why would a rent-to-own company need to be in your community?

It's about relationships. You want to work with someone you feel you can trust. You want to be able to meet with them in person and know that you're in good hands. There's a lot more trust and accountability between two people who can shake hands, look one another in the eye, and know that both parties are invested in the outcome.

You also want someone who knows the area, the real estate

market, and the community. Where you buy a home has a lot to do with the schools, the neighbors, and the value of the surrounding properties, too. A local company will know the history of the area and the value of your potential new home.

And what if there is a problem? You need to be able to meet with people and get things sorted out. After all, during the rental phase, the rent-to-own company owns the home. What do you do if something goes wrong and they're not available to help you?

How to Avoid Making This Mistake:

When you're looking for a rent-to-own company, look locally first. Find a reputable organization, meet with the staff, and really strives to create a rent-to-own deal that works for you.

(Check out our website and contact information on the back cover, and fill out your no-obligation application today.)

Rent to Own Mistake #8: Not Working With a Complete Rent-to-Own TEAM

There are many things that can go wrong with a rent-to-own deal. If you want your home to be the best home possible, if you want to have good credit by the time you've saved your down payment, if you want to have a legally binding and comprehensive rent-to-own agreement, and if you want to have quality representation as you navigate the mortgage process, then you need a complete team behind you.

A R2O Pro with a complete team provides the following members and support:

A Real Estate Agent – to help you find the best home that fits your needs and your budget.

A Property Inspector – to be sure your future home is in good shape. You want to know any potential issues before you close the deal.

A Lawyer – to prepare and review the appropriate documentation and make sure that everything is legal and binding, and to help answer any questions you might have about the agreement.

A Credit Repair Specialist – to help you understand your current financial situation, create an action plan to repair your credit, and to provide follow-ups and support as you work toward qualifying for a mortgage and eventually purchasing your home.

A Mortgage Broker – to coordinate the financing for you to buy the home.

As you can see, there are a number of important team members who will be involved in the process to help you navigate and succeed with your rent-to-own deal.

When you are working with a private home-seller, or an inexperienced investor, chances are they're working on their own. They don't have a team, and that means you don't have experts and specialty people behind you, helping you along the way.

Ultimately that means that you may suffer. Details can be missed and homes can be lost.

If you're going to work hard and go through the rent-to-own process, you want to make sure that you have a good team working hard for you.

How to Avoid Making This Mistake:

You have two choices here.

You can hire your own experts. You can hire a lawyer, a home inspector, a credit repair specialist and more. You can build your own team. It's expensive and time consuming, however it is important enough that if you're doing a private deal, it's worth the time and expense.

Or

You can work with a ready-made team of specialists who are all dedicated to helping you get into your own home. They know what they're doing and they have your back. Your success is their success, and they'll work hard to make your home ownership dreams come true. That's what working with a quality R2O Pro is all about.

(Check out our website and contact information on the back cover, and fill out your no-obligation application today.)

Rent to Own Mistake #9: Not Having a Road Map or a Plan

Have you ever headed out on a road trip? You're excited about the destination, right? But you wouldn't pack up the car and start driving without a map, or without a plan.

You need to know what roads to take to get to your destination.

You need to know how long the trip will take and where you'll stop along the way.

You'll plan for food, fuel, and sleep.

The same is true for the rent-to-own process.

Your destination is home ownership, and you need to have a plan to get from where you are now to owning your home.

Unlike a road trip, the process of renting to own is an involved process. It takes many people to pull it all together, and if these people aren't all following the same plan, well, you can get off course.

And let's be upfront here and say that buying a home is a big deal.

Buying a home is something that you will be both financially and emotionally invested in. Your family members are impacted as well. If something goes wrong, money can be lost and people can be disappointed. You can be disappointed.

Every part of the process needs to follow a plan. Every step must be performed properly from the very beginning so that it all falls into place.

That is why having a rock-solid plan from the beginning is so important.

Your road map begins by making sure...

- That the home you're looking at meets your current needs.

- That it will also meet your future needs.

- The home is structurally safe, and in a safe area.

- The home doesn't have any significant issues that could surprise you later on.

- Your current financial situation is clearly understood.

- Your time frame from rental to ownership makes sense, based on your financial needs and goals.

- Your rent-to-own paperwork is 100% legal and above board.

- You understand what you're signing and everyone is on the same page. Everyone agrees on the terms and understands them.

The bottom line is that you need a road map and a solid plan to take you from where you are right now to the day you're sitting in your own home.

How to Avoid Making This Mistake:

Just knowing the potential mistakes that many rent-to-own clients make can help you navigate the process successfully and create a top level rent-to-own deal.

You have the knowledge and information to get started today. You can take what you've learned and create your own rent-to-own deal.

Or you can hire a great rent-to-own company and R2O Pro to set it all up for you. They can help you shorten the process so you're in your own home sooner than you thought possible!

(Check out our website and contact information on the back cover, and fill out your no-obligation application today.)

My home...it is my retreat and resting place..."

-Michel de Montaigne

Frequently Asked Questions

How Long Does Rent To Own Take?

The entire process from application to home ownership generally takes three years. It can take a little longer, depending on your needs. That said, time flies! Just imagine, three short years from now your credit is in good shape, you own a home, and you're living the dream!

I've Filled Out The Application, When Will I Hear Back?

You'll hear back from one of our representatives in a few business days. If you don't hear back from us, there may be a technical error and we didn't receive your application. Give us a call! We're always happy to speak with you.

(Check out our website and contact information on the back cover)

I'm Having Trouble Finding A House That I Like, What Should I Do?

Be patient and review your list of priorities. While you shouldn't buy a house that you don't like, sometimes you may have a wish list that is larger than what's available within your budget.

Keep in mind that your first home doesn't have to be your forever home. You can use that equity that we talked about to spruce it up, sell it and make money on the deal. Then you can buy your perfect forever home.

OR

You can make the changes that you want to your home and create your perfect home.

Can I Make Repairs And Improvements During The Rental Phase?

In many cases, you can make minor changes to the home, like painting walls. Keep in mind that you're on the path to repair your credit and saving a down payment, so it doesn't make sense to spend your money on expensive repairs or improvements.

When you own the home, then you can begin making more significant changes.

Can You Really Help Me Repair My Credit?

Yes, and we take great pride in that. It's our goal to make

sure that when it comes time to apply for your mortgage, you're practically guaranteed to qualify.

We want you to succeed, and that means coming up with a credit repair plan for you and helping you along the way.

Is Rent to Own for Everyone? What if I Don't Qualify?

Rent to own isn't for everyone. You do have to meet certain criteria and not everyone will qualify. If you don't qualify, we'll be happy to explain why. There may be some simple steps you can take to qualify for rent to own, and then you can re-apply.

You won't know until you fill out the application and try. Today may be the first positive step you take to owning your own home. You have nothing to lose and everything to gain.

What if I Don't have the 5% Option Fee to Get Started?

Generally speaking, as long as you have a good family income and are serious about getting into your own home rather than renting, we can probably help you out.

The "Option Fee" we require applies towards your down payment when you eventually buy the home from us. In some cases, we can work with as little as $2,000 to get started, and we can help. We offer financing and trade opportunities to help you come up with the rest. Our goal is to help you get into your home sooner rather than later!

What's Next?

The purpose of this book is to give you a very good understanding of the pro's and con's of doing a rent-to-own deal.

Buying a home (either the traditional way, or through a rent-to-own process) is the single biggest investment most of us will ever make. It's important that you have a clear understanding of how it all works, and what the possible pitfalls are.

Thanks to quality rent-to-own companies and R2O Pros, the dream of home ownership is now within the grasp of hundreds of thousands of good people who 'don't quite qualify' for mortgages with the picky big banks.

Are you ready? Would you like to take that step towards becoming a home owner?

Great!

Let us help you to get into the home of your dreams FAST (even if the banks have said 'no').

Go ahead and check out our website and contact information on the back cover, and fill out your no-obligation application today!

Home ownership for you and your family can be just a click or phone call away!